Super
Shred

Diet Recipes Ready In 30 Minutes

74 Mouthwatering Main Courses, Stews & Smoothie Recipes Inside!

SHARON STEWART

Legal & Disclaimer

The information contained in this book is not designed to replace or take the place of any form of medicine or professional medical advice. The information in this book has been provided for educational and entertainment purposes only

The information contained in this book has been compiled from sources deemed reliable and it is accurate to the best of the Author's knowledge; however, the Author cannot guarantee its accuracy and validity and cannot be held liable for any errors or omissions. Changes are periodically made to this book. You must consult your doctor or get professional medical advice before using any of the suggested remedies, techniques or information in this book.

Upon using the information contained in this book, you agree to hold harmless the Author from and against any damages, costs and expenses, including any legal fees, potentially resulting from the application of any of the information provided by this guide. This disclaimer applies to any damages or injury caused by the use and application, whether directly or indirectly, of any advice or information presented, whether for breach of contract, tort, negligence, personal injury, criminal intent or under any other cause of action.

You agree to accept all risk of using the information presented inside this book. You need to consult a professional medical practitioner in order to ensure you are both able & healthy enough to participate in this program.

Table of Contents

Introduction... 7

    How To Get Started? 7

Chapter 1 Mouthwatering Super SHRED Recipes 9

    Main Courses Recipes Ready Under 30 Minutes 9

      Beef Stir-Fry 9

      Ham and Cheese Egg Scramble 10

      Chicken and Green Eggs 11

      Lobster Boat 11

      Turkey Swiss melt 12

      Brown Rice and Chicken Stew 12

      Black Beans and Mixed Vegetables 13

      Baked Tilapia with Broccoli 13

      Sage Pesto with Roasted Yellow Summer Squash 14

      Watercress Salad with Sardines 15

      Vegetable Medley 15

      Sweet Potato Frittata 16

      Ukrainian Beef and Eggs 17

      Green Bean Chicken 17

      Lemon Garlic Shrimp 18

      Yogurt and Cucumber Salad 19

      Grilled Chicken with Rosemary, Sage, and Garlic 19

      Halibut with Cilantro Garlic Sauce 20

      Parmesan Encrusted Zucchini 21

      Mixed Cauliflower Rice with Sumac and Onions 21

      Chicken Meatball Noodle Bowl 22

      Buttered Salmon 23

      Vegetable Fish Bowl 23

      Mexican Beef and Tortilla Combo 24

      Grilled Turkey Panini 25

      Spicy Beef Noodle 25

      Crusted Cod Fish Fillet 26

      Gingered Beef with Broccoli 27

Fried Rice with Cuban Flavors 27
Triple Mango Grilled Chicken 28
Grilled Tilapia with Chutney 29
Quinoa and Avocado Dinner 29
Open Face Veggie Burger 30
Healthy Grilled Cheese 31
Chicken Fajitas with Pineapple 32
Grilled Spinach Cheese Pizza 32
Beef and Bean Chili 33
Black Bean Rice 34
Buttered Sirloin Steak 34
Baked Spinach and Pita 35
Baked & Buttered Haddock 36
Grilled Halibut Steaks 36
Low Fat Pasta with Asparagus 37
Spicy Chicken with Mushrooms 38
Trout Fillets in Foil 39
Quick and Easy Garlic Pasta 39
15-minute Tuna Melts 40
Stir Fry Beef Asian-Style 41
Broiled Herbed Chicken 41
Steak and Spinach Salad with Walnuts 42

Soups and Stews Recipes Ready Under 30 Minutes 43
Chicken Noodle Soup 43
Bean, Rice, and Chicken Stew 44
Corn Chowder 44
Black Bean Soup 45
Sweet Potato Carrot Soup 46
White Bean Soup 46
Tomato Bisque Soup 47
Classic Lentil Soup 48
Gazpacho Soup 48
Chickpea Soup 49

Snacks 50
150-Calorie Snacks 50
100-Calorie Snacks 53

Super SHRED Fruit Smoothies and Protein Shake Recipes Ready Under 30 Minutes 56
Blast of Super Protein Shake 56
Splash of the Tropics Protein Shake 57

Chocolate-y Protein Shake 57
Very Berry Protein Shake 58
Red Revolution Protein Shake 58
Peach and Strawberry Smoothie 59
Creamy Delight Smoothie 59
Berry Lemon Smoothie 60
Easy-Peasy Mango Smoothie 60
Berry-Orange Twist Smoothie 61
Sweet Detoxification Smoothie 61
Super Green Smoothie 62
The Energizer Pear-Blueberry Smoothie 62
Cucumber Delight Smoothie 63

Chapter 2 The Super SHRED Diet Crash Course For Beginners 64

What Is The Super SHRED Diet? 64

How does the Super SHRED Diet Work? 64

Guidelines for a Successful SHRED Program 66

4 Phases of the SUPER SHRED Diet 68

Week 1: Foundation 68
Week 2: Accelerate 70
Week 3: Shape 70
Week 4: Tenacious 71

Chapter 3 Jumpstart Your Super SHRED Diet! 73

7-Day Sample Meal Template 73

Week 1, Day 1 73
Week 1, Day 2 75
Week 1, Day 3 76
Week 1, Day 4 78
Week 1, Day 5 79
Week 1, Day 6 80
Week 1, Day 7 82

Preparing Yourself 84

Your Daily Motivation Guide 84

Conclusion 85

Check Out Other Books 86

"Beverly is a 54-year old woman who started the Super SHRED diet when she found herself on a plateau after losing 40 pounds. She went on the Super SHRED program in August, and by December of the same year, she found herself 45 pounds lighter. In addition, her blood cholesterol dropped from her highest number of 265 down to 188. She now wears a size 16/18 which is down from a whopping size of 24/26. According to her, SHREDding taught her how to make healthy food choices, and now it has become her way of life."

Introduction

The Super SHRED Diet Recipes Quick & Easy guide is designed to help you jump right into losing weight using the Super SHRED Diet, right from the start.

Unlike other Super SHRED Diet books, this is the only guide designed for busy working professionals with families.

As we explore further, you'll get:

- 20 Step-By-Step Mouthwatering Main Course Recipes Ready Under 30 Minutes

- 10 Step-By-Step Delicious Soups & Stews

- A List of Super SHRED-friendly 150-calories Snacks

- A List of Super SHRED-friendly 100-calories Snacks

- 14 Step-By-Step Super SHRED Fruit Smoothies & Protein Shakes

In addition, you'll also receive the *Super Shred Diet Crash Course For Beginners* (Chapter 2) and the *7-Day Sample Meal Template* (Chapter 3) to jumpstart your weight loss... starting in just minutes from now.

How To Get Started?

If you're a complete beginner with the Super SHRED Diet, then I suggest you to skip to Chapter 2.

If you're familiar with the diet and you're just looking for recipes, then simply turn the pages and jumpstart your weight loss right away!

CHAPTER 1

Mouthwatering Super SHRED Recipes

Main Courses Recipes Ready Under 30 Minutes

In this section, you'll get 20 recipes that could be easily prepared by anyone – whether you are first-timers or veteran cookers.

I'm sure you'll love the short preparation process because I've deliberately selected a wide range of universal recipes that could be prepared in as short as 10 minutes to 30 minutes. (Yes, it is possible!)

So are you ready? Let's get cookin'!

Beef Stir-Fry

Serves 2

Calories: *208 calories per serving*

Ingredients:

- 4 oz. Lean ground beef,
- ¼ medium Onion, sliced
- ½ medium Green bell pepper, sliced
- ½ medium Red bell pepper, sliced
- ½ tbsp. Crushed chili pepper,
- ½ tbsp. Sesame seeds, roasted
- ½ tbsp. Balsamic vinegar

Preparation:

Brown the ground beef in a skillet then add the onions and peppers followed by the vinegar and sesame seeds and continue to heat in the skillet. Serve once beef is cooked and tender.

Ham and Cheese Egg Scramble

Serves 2

Calories: *200 calories per serving*

Ingredients:

- 1 whole egg, and 1 egg white
- 1-2 slices Low-fat ham
- 1 slice Low-fat cheese

Preparation:

1. In a non-stick skillet, cook ham until lightly browned.

2. Next add the scrambled eggs and cheese then cook while stirring frequently until the eggs are done. Serve hot.

Chicken and Green Eggs

Serves 1

Calories: *300 calories*

Ingredients:

- 1 large egg
- 3 oz. Chicken breast
- ¼ cup Chopped broccoli
- ½ cup Raw baby spinach
- ½ tbsp. Olive oil

Preparation:

1. In a non-stick skillet, brown the chicken in olive oil.
2. When it's halfway done, add broccoli and continue to cook.
3. After the chicken is thoroughly cooked, add the eggs and spinach then thoroughly combine until everything is done. Serve hot.

Lobster Boat

Serves 2

Calories: *260 calories per serving*

Ingredients:

- 6-8 oz. Lobster
- 1 tbsp. Light mayo
- Juice from ¼ lemon
- ¼ Bell pepper, sliced
- ¼ Onion, sliced
- 1 Celery stalk
- 3-4 Romaine lettuce heart leaves
- Salt and pepper to taste

Preparation:

1. Place the lobster meat in a bowl then add diced vegetables.
2. Mix in the mayo, lemon juice, and spices.
3. Fill each romaine lettuce leaf with the lobster salad. Serve.

Turkey Swiss melt

Serves 2

Calories: *170 calories per serving*

Ingredients:

- 2 slices Low-fat deli turkey breast
- 1 slice Low-fat Swiss cheese
- ½ small Avocado
- ½ tsp. Olive oil
- Salt and pepper to taste

Preparation:

1. Add oil to a pan over medium-heat then lay the turkey slices on top of the oil.
2. Place one strip of cheese and one avocado slice on top of each turkey breast.
3. Roll into a tube and flip over to brown the other side. Cheese should be slightly melted and the avocado should be soft.
4. Season with salt and pepper to taste.

Brown Rice and Chicken Stew

Serves 2

Calories: *200 calories per serving*

Ingredients:

- 1 cup Brown rice, cooked
- 8 oz. Chicken
- 1 cup Sweet kernel corn
- 1 cup Black beans
- ½ cup Chicken broth,
- 2 tbsp. Barbeque sauce
- ¼ Onion, chopped

Preparation:

Stir everything together in a pan over medium heat until the onions are cooked. Serve warm.

Black Beans and Mixed Vegetables

Serves 2

Calories: *200 calories per serving*

Ingredients:

- 1 cup Mixed vegetables
- ½ cup Black beans, cooked
- ½ tsp. Butter
- ½ tsp. Salt-Free Mrs. Dash
- Salt and pepper to taste

Preparation:

1. Add 2 tbsp. of water to a microwavable bowl then add the mixed vegetables.

2. Cover and microwave for 5-6 minutes then drain the water after cooking.

3. Wash black beans and add to the bowl along with Mrs. Dash.

4. Cook until beans are done. Season with salt and pepper to taste.

Baked Tilapia with Broccoli

Serves 1

Calories: *160 calories per serving*

Ingredients:

- 4 oz. Tilapia
- 8 oz. Broccoli
- 1/8 tsp. Salt
- 1/8 tsp. Pepper
- 1 tsp. Lemon juice
- 1/8 tsp. Basil, dried

Preparation:

1. Heat oven to 350° C.

2. Spray a piece of aluminum foil with no-calorie cooking spray then place fish on it and season with salt, pepper, and basil.

3. Top with broccoli, drizzle with lemon juice, then fold the foil to make a packet.

4. Bake for 20 minutes until fish flakes with a fork.

5. Sprinkle with parmesan cheese if desired, and serve hot.

Sage Pesto with Roasted Yellow Summer Squash

Serves 4

Calories: *80 calories per serving*

Ingredients:

- 6 Summer squash, washed and cubed
- 1 tbsp. Extra virgin olive oil
- ¼ cup Sage-pecan Pesto
- Salt and pepper to taste

Preparation:

1. Preheat oven to 400° F.

2. Toss squash with olive oil and season with salt and pepper.

3. Arrange the squash slices in a roasting pan then roast in the oven for 25-30 minutes until squash begins to brown at the sides.

4. Allow to cool then toss with pesto.

5. Serve.

Watercress Salad with Sardines

Serves 2

Calories: *200 calories per serving*

Ingredients:

- Zest and juice of 1 lemon
- 1 tbsp. Olive oil
- 2 cups Watercress sprigs
- ¼ small Red onion, chopped
- 1 tbsp. fresh Tarragon
- 2 Clementines
- 1 (4-oz.) can Olive-oil packed sardines
- 3 tbsp. Pumpkin seeds, toasted
- Vinaigrette
- Coarse salt and pepper

Preparation:

Whisk olive oil and lemon zest in a bowl until thoroughly combined then season with salt and pepper. Arrange watercress, red onions, and tarragon on a platter. Top with clementines, sardines, and pumpkin seeds. Season with salt and pepper and drizzle with vinaigrette to taste.

Vegetable Medley

Serves 6

Calories: *200 calories per serving*

Ingredients:

- 1 tbsp. Olive oil
- 2 Yellow squash, diced
- 2 Zucchini, diced

- 1 Onion, chopped
- 1 Green bell pepper
- 2 Garlic cloves, crushed

- 1 (16 oz.) can Tomatoes, diced
- 2 tbsp. Oregano, dried
- ½ tsp. Basil, dried
- Salt and pepper to taste

Preparation:

Pre-heat oven to 325° F. In a large skillet, heat olive oil over medium heat. Add squash, onions, zucchini, green bell peppers, and garlic. Sauté until all the vegetables are tender. Serve warm.

Sweet Potato Frittata

Serves 1

Calories: *200 calories*

Ingredients:

- 2 large Eggs
- ½ large Sweet potato, baked
- 1½ slices Lean turkey bacon
- 1/8 cup Shredded cheese
- ½ tbsp. Low-fat sour cream

Preparation:

Remove the sweet potato peel and mash the flesh. Reheat in the microwave or in a skillet. In a separate pan, cook turkey bacon until done. Pour the eggs on top and allow to cook until set. Sprinkle grated cheese on top then add sweet potato mash to the egg mixture. Serve with sour cream on top.

Ukrainian Beef and Eggs

Serves 2

Calories: *250 calories per serving*

Ingredients:

- 3 Eggs, scrambled
- 4 oz. Lean ground beef
- 1/8 cup Reduced-fat shredded cheese
- ½ cup Reduced-fat Greek yogurt
- 2 cups Spinach
- ½ Onion

Preparation:

Brown the ground beef in a skillet over medium heat, add chopped onions, and pour scrambled eggs into the skillet over beef and onions. Once they start to thicken, add spinach, and combine well. When the eggs are firm and the spinach has reduced, top with cheese and Greek yogurt, and serve.

Green Bean Chicken

Serves 4

Calories: *300 Calories per serving*

Ingredients:

- 2 tbsp. Olive oil
- 3 cloves Garlic
- 1 pound Chicken breast halves, skinless, boneless, and cubed
- 2 oz. canned Tomatoes, diced
- 2 tbsp. fresh Basil
- 1 pound fresh Green beans, steamed

Preparation:

Heat olive oil in a large skillet over medium heat then add garlic and sauté until aromatic oils are released. Add the chicken and cook thoroughly then add tomatoes and basil and bring to a boil. Reduce heat to low and simmer for a couple of minutes then add steamed beans and serve warm.

Lemon Garlic Shrimp

Serves 4

Calories: *100 calories per serving*

Ingredients:

- 2 tbsp. Olive oil
- 1 tbsp. Butter
- 2 tbsp. Garlic, minced
- 2 tbsp. Lemon juice
- 1 tbsp. Lemon zest
- Sea salt to taste

Preparation:

In a skillet, melt butter over medium heat. Add the shrimp in a single layer and cook just until they turn pink, – no longer than 1-2 minutes. Turn the shrimp over and add the minced garlic. Continue to cook until shrimp are slightly firm. Remove from heat then add lemon juice, lemon zest, and salt. Serve immediately.

Yogurt and Cucumber Salad

Serves 4

Calories: *80 Calories per serving*

Ingredients:

- 2 Cucumbers, sliced
- ¾ cup fresh Dill
- ½ cup Greek yogurt
- ½ cup Feta cheese, crumbled
- Salt & Black pepper to taste

Preparation:

Wash dill and then add to the cucumbers in a medium to large mixing bowl. Combine then stir in the yogurt making sure all the cucumbers are coated with yogurt. Once thoroughly mixed, and gently fold in the feta cheese. Do not over mix. Serve cold.

Grilled Chicken with Rosemary, Sage, and Garlic

Serves 4

Calories: *210 Calories per serving*

Ingredients:

- 4 Chicken breasts, boneless and skinless
- 2 tbsp. Sage,
- 1 tsp. dried Rosemary,
- 2 tbsp. White wine vinegar
- 5 tbsp. Extra-virgin olive oil
- 1 tsp. Dijon mustard
- 1 tsp. garlic, minced

Preparation:

Mix all herbs, vinegar, and oil in a bowl, then transfer mixture to a mortar and pestle and grind well. Rub about 2 tbsp. of the dry mixture on the chicken breasts. Seal inside a Ziploc bag or another leak-proof container and marinate overnight. When ready to prepare, spray a grill with nonstick cooking oil or spray then cook chicken 4-5 minutes on each side. Flip when it feels firm to the touch and is lightly brown. When both sides are done, and serve hot .

Halibut with Cilantro Garlic Sauce

Serves 4

Calories: *160 per serving*

Ingredients:

- 4 Garlic cloves
- 1 cup Chicken stock
- 2 tsp. Lime zest
- 2 Limes
- 4 tbsp. Olive oil
- 3 tbsp. fresh Cilantro, chopped

Preparation:

Sauté garlic in olive oil in a skillet over medium heat. Next add lime zest and chicken stock then simmer for 10 minutes until stock is reduced. Stir in cilantro and lime juice. Brush each side of fish with the sauce then grill until both sides are firm to the touch. Serve immediately.

Parmesan Encrusted Zucchini

Serves 4

Calories: *130 calories per serving*

Ingredients:

- 4 Zucchinis
- 2/3 cup Parmesan cheese, grated
- 1 tbsp. Butter
- Salt to taste

Preparation:

Cut zucchini into French fry style slices.
Bring salted water to a boil, add zucchini slices, and cook until they become tender. Once cooked, remove from heat, drain, and place in an ice bath. Next, dry zucchini completely and layer in a roasting pan. Sprinkle with grated parmesan and roast in the oven for about 15 minutes. Serve immediately.

Mixed Cauliflower Rice with Sumac and Onions

Serves 2

Calories: *150 calories per serving*

Ingredients:

- 1 tbsp. Olive oil
- 1 small Onion
- ½ head Cauliflower, chopped and grated in a food processor
- Salt and pepper to taste
- Sumac to taste

Preparation:

Heat olive oil in a skillet, add onions and sauté. Once brown, add cauliflower, and season with salt and pepper. Cook for no more than 5 minutes, then sprinkle with Sumac to taste and serve.

Chicken Meatball Noodle Bowl

Serves 2

Calories: *358 calories per serving*

Ingredients:

- 2 oz. thin rice noodles
- 6 oz. ground chicken
- 1/2 tbsp. fresh ginger, grated
- 1 tbsp. fresh cilantro, chopped
- 1/4 tsp. salt
- 1 red chili pepper, seeded and chopped
- 1 tbsp. honey
- 1/2 tbsp. lime juice
- 1 1/2 cups lettuce, shredded
- 1/4 cup carrot, shredded
- 1/8 cup rice vinegar

Preparation:

1. Cook noodles according to package instructions. Drain and set aside

2. In a large bowl, combine chicken, salt, cilantro and ginger. Mix well and shape into meatballs.

3. Spray baking sheet with cooking oil spray then bake meatballs for 10 minutes on one side and another 10 minutes for the other side or until cooked.

4. In a small bowl, mix honey, vinegar, lime juice and chili pepper. Set aside.

5. Divide vegetables and noodles into two bowls. Top with meatballs and drizzle with sauce.

Buttered Salmon

Serves 2

Calories: *294 calories per serving*

Ingredients:

- 2 fresh or frozen salmon, skinless
- 1 tbsp. butter, softened
- 1/4 tsp. lemon-pepper seasoning
- 1/2 tsp. fresh basil, crushed
- 1/2 tsp. fresh parsley, chopped
- 1/8 tsp. lemon peel, shredded

Preparation:

1. Rinse fish and pat dry with paper towel. Season with salt-free lemon-pepper seasoning.

2. Transfer fish on a greased rack of a broiler pan. Place about 4 inches from heat and broil for 5 minutes. Broil for 5 to 7 minutes to cook other side or until flaky.

3. In a bowl, combine butter and the rest of ingredients. Spoon butter mixture and top on each fish then serve.

Vegetable Fish Bowl

Serves 2

Calories: *264 calories per serving*

Ingredients:

- 1/2 lb white fish, cut into 2 pieces
- 1 1/8 cup water
- 1/2 of 14-oz. can vegetable broth
- 1/2 of 4-oz. package mashed potato

- 1 carrot, thinly sliced
- 1/2 cup sugar snap peas, halves
- 1/2 tbsp. olive oil
- salt and black pepper to taste

Preparation:

1. Season the fish with pepper. Place in a Dutch oven and cook together carrots and peas in olive oil for 3 minutes.

2. Stir in broth and water then bring to a boil. Reduce heat and simmer for 3 minutes with cover.

3. In a bowl, transfer mashed potatoes. Carefully scoop about 3/4 cups of broth into the potatoes or until thick.

4. Divide potatoes into two bowls. Break fish and transfer chowder over mashed potatoes the season with salt and pepper to taste.

Mexican Beef and Tortilla Combo

Serves 2

Calories: *319 calories per serving*

Ingredients:

- 4 6-in tortillas
- 1/2 lb leftover lean beef roast
- 1/2 of 14-oz can diced tomatoes
- 1/2 green pepper, chopped in strips
- fresh cilantro

Preparation:

1. Wrap tortillas in paper towels and nuke for 60 seconds at 100% high. Set aside.

2. Nuke leftover lean beef roast until warm. In a saucepan, place tomatoes and heat.

3. Slice meat and serve on top of tortillas together with tomatoes and green pepper.

Grilled Turkey Panini

Serves 2

Calories: *348 calories per serving*

Ingredients:

- 4 slices whole wheat Italian bread
- 6 oz. sliced turkey breast, cooked
- 1/2 cup spinach leaves
- 1/4 cup classic bruschetta topper
- 1 tbsp. mayonnaise
- olive oil

Preparation:

- Spread 2 slices of bread with bruschetta topper then layer with turkey and spinach.
- Spread mayo on remaining bread slices and top on turkey and spinach layers.
- In a hot skillet, grill bread for 2 minutes. Turn and grill for another 2 minutes.

Spicy Beef Noodle

Serves 2

Calories: *316 calories per serving*

Ingredients:

- 1/2 lb. lean beef, cut in strips
- 3/4 cup egg noodles
- 1 cup broccoli florets
- 1 14-oz. can reduced sodium beef broth
- 3 tbsp. bottled peanut sauce

Preparation:

1. In a Dutch oven, cook beef in 2 tablespoons of broth over medium high. Add the rest of the broth and peanut sauce. Bring to a boil.

2. Add noodles, reduce heat and simmer uncovered for 4 minutes.

3. Add broccoli and bring to a boil. Reduce heat, simmer uncovered for another 4 minutes.

4. Divide beef and noodle into two bowls then serve.

Crusted Cod Fish Fillet

Serves 2

Calories: *230 calories per serving*

Ingredients:

- 2 skinless cod fillets
- 3 tbsp. panko bread crumbs
- 1 1/2 cups carrots, julienned
- 1/3 cup Parmesan cheese, shredded
- 1/4 cup water
- 1/2 tsp. ground fresh ginger
- 1/2 tbsp. butter
- mixed fresh salad greens
- salt and pepper to taste

Preparation:

1. Preheat oven to 450 degrees F. Spray baking sheet with cooking spray.

2. Rinse and dry fish, place in baking sheet and season with salt and pepper.

3. In a bowl, combine bread crumbs and cheese. Coat fish with mixture and bake for 4 to 6 minutes per half inch of cod fillets.

4. While baking, boil water in a skillet. Add carrots then reduce heat and cook covered for 5 minutes.

5. Remove cover and cook for another 2 minutes. Stir in butter and ginger.

6. Serve fish together with carrots and salad greens.

Gingered Beef with Broccoli

Serves 2

Calories: *237 calories per serving*

Ingredients:

- 6 oz. beef sirloin steak
- 4 cups mixed baby salad greens
- 1 1/2 cups broccoli florets
- 1/2 red pepper
- 80 ml ginger vinaigrette salad dressing

Preparation:

1. Remove fat from beef then slice thinly into bite-size strips. Set aside.

2. In a skillet, heat 2 tablespoon of the dressing, add broccoli and cook for 3 minutes over medium high heat.

3. Stir in beef and cook for 3 minutes. Remove beef and broccoli and set aside. Cut pepper into strips.

4. In a bowl, combine salad greens, beef, broccoli and pepper. Drizzle with the remaining dressing, mix and serve.

Fried Rice with Cuban Flavors

Serves 4

Calories: *375 calories per serving*

Ingredients:

- 12 oz. cooked turkey, chopped
- 1 cup sweet peppers, chopped
- 3/4 cup black beans, rinsed and drained
- 1 fresh pineapple, peeled
- 1 oz. long green rice, cooked
- 1 jalapeno pepper, chopped
- 1 tbsp. olive oil

Preparation:

1. Cut pineapple into bite size slices and reserve juice.
2. In a skillet, heat oil, add pineapple and cook for 4 minutes over medium high heat.
3. In a skillet, cook ham and pepper for 3 minutes. Add beans and cooked rice. Cook for another 3 minutes while stirring occasionally.
4. Add pineapple juice and serve topped with pineapple slices.

Triple Mango Grilled Chicken

Serves 2
Calories: *257 calories per serving*

Ingredients:

- 2 boneless chicken breasts, halves and skinless
- 1 mango, peeled and cubed
- 1 zucchini, thinly sliced
- 1/4 cup mango fruit drink
- 1/8 cup mango chutney
- 1 tbsp. olive oil
- salt and pepper

Preparation:

- Season the chicken with salt and pepper. Grill chicken for 6 minutes on each side or until cooked.
- In a skillet, add mango cubes, mango drink and chutney. Simmer for 3 minutes stirring occasionally.
- To cook zucchini, place in a square dish with 14 cups water. Nuke for 2 to 3 minutes at 100% high. Drain and place chicken on top of zucchini.

Grilled Tilapia with Chutney

Serves 4

Calories: *304 calories per serving*

Ingredients:

- 4 oz. skinless tilapia
- 1 cup green grapes
- 1/2 cup mixed dried fruit bits
- 1/3 cup apricot fruit
- 1/3 cup sliced green onions
- salt and black pepper

Preparation:

- Rinse and pat dry tilapia then season with salt and pepper.
- Grill fish for 3 minutes or until the fish is flaky. Turn and cook for 2 to 3 minutes. Place fish in a serving plate
- In a skillet, add grapes, fruits bits, apricot and green onions. Cook for 2 minutes and season with salt and pepper. Serve over fish.

Quinoa and Avocado Dinner

Serves 4

Calories: *322 calories per serving*

Ingredients:

- 1 cup water
- 1/2 cup uncooked quinoa
- 1/2 cup fresh spinach, shredded
- 1/3 cup feta cheese, crumbled
- 1/3 cup red onion, chopped
- 2 Roma tomatoes, chopped
- 2 ripe avocados, sliced
- 2 tbsp. olive oil
- 2 tbsp. lemon juice
- 1/2 salt

Preparation:

1. In a saucepan, combine water and rinsed quinoa. Bring to a boil, reduce heat and simmer with cover for 15 minutes.

2. Transfer in a bowl then add onion, spinach and tomato.

3. In a bowl, combine olive oil, salt and lemon juice. Whisk until combined then add to quinoa.

4. In 4 plates, arrange avocado slices and top with divided quinoa. Sprinkle with feta cheese and serve.

Open Face Veggie Burger

Serves 2

Calories: *329 calories per serving*

Ingredients:

- 2 frozen veggie burgers
- 1 1/2 cups sweet onion, thinly sliced
- 1/2 cup baby spinach leaves
- 2 slices whole wheat bread
- 1 tbsp. steak sauce
- 1 tbsp. mayonnaise
- 1 tbsp. olive oil
- 1/2 tsp. yellow mustard

Preparation:

1. In a skillet, heat olive oil, add onion slices and cook for 10 minutes over medium high heat. Stir in steak sauce.

2. Prepare veggie burgers according to package instructions.

3. In a bowl, combine mayo and mustard. Spread on one side of bread slices. Layer the burger and spinach on bread slices.

4. Spoon onion and top on burgers then serve.

Healthy Grilled Cheese

Serves 2

Calories: *359 calories per serving*

Ingredients:

- 6 slices whole grain bread, toasted
- 3 oz. fresh mozzarella cheese, chopped
- 1 1/2 cup fresh baby spinach leaves
- 1 cup pickled mixed vegetables
- 1/4 cup oil-packed dried tomatoes
- 1/4 tsp. ground pepper
- 1/2 tsp. minced garlic

Preparation:

1. Rinse and drain pickled vegetables. Transfer in a large bowl and add all ingredients except bread slices.

2. Microwave for 2 minutes without the cover until cheese begins to melt.

3. To make the sandwiches, layer the veggie and cheese mixture on 2 slices of bread. Top with another bread and layer with cheese mixture again. Finish off with the remaining bread slices.

Chicken Fajitas with Pineapple

Serves 4

Calories: *393 calories per serving*

Ingredients:

- 1 whole egg, and 1 egg white
- 1-2 slices Low-fat ham
- 1 slice Low-fat cheese

Preparation:

1. Preheat oven to 350 degrees F and heat tortillas wrapped in foil in the oven.

2. Spray skillet with cooking spray. Add pineapple slices and cook for 5 minutes over medium high heat. Remove and set aside.

3. In a skillet, heat oil and toss chicken, peppers and jerk seasoning. Cook for 5 minutes or until chicken is cooked.

4. Slice pineapple into bite size pieces. Serve with chicken and tortillas.

Grilled Spinach Cheese Pizza

Serves 8

Calories: *340 calories per serving*

Ingredients:

- 4 oz. chicken breast, cooked and chopped
- 1 cup Alfredo sauce
- 1 cup Mozzarella cheese, shredded
- 10-oz frozen spinach, chopped
- 1 lb refrigerated pizza dough
- 2 tbsp. olive oil
- 1 tsp. red pepper, crushed

Preparation:

1. Preheat grill to medium heat.

2. In a sauce pan, cook Alfredo sauce for 4 minutes over medium heat. Add pepper and spinach.

3. Divide pizza dough into 4 equal pieces. Roll the dough on a floured surface then brush with a tablespoon of oil.

4. Grill dough with oil side down for 5 minutes or until golden brown. Brush with remaining oil and turn.

5. While grilling, top the dough with spinach, cheese and chicken mixture. Grill for another 5 to 7 minutes or until cheese melts.

Beef and Bean Chili

Serves 4

Calories: *266 calories per serving*

Ingredients:

- 13 oz. lean ground beef
- 3/4 15-oz can kidney beans
- 3/4 15-oz. can diced tomatoes
- 3/4 of package chili seasoning mix

Preparation:

1. In a skillet, cook beef until browned over medium high heat.

2. Remove grease then add tomatoes, kidney beans and seasoning mix. Reduce heat and simmer for 15 minutes. Serve and enjoy!

Black Bean Rice

Serves 4

Calories: *240 calories per serving*

Ingredients:

- 1 cup low sodium vegetable broth
- 1/2 cup uncooked white rice
- 1 1/2 cup canned black beans, drained
- 1 tsp. ground cumin
- 1 tsp. olive oil
- 1 onion, chopped
- 1 clove garlic, minced
- 1/4 tsp. cayenne pepper

Preparation:

1. In a pot, heat oil over medium high heat. Stir in onion and garlic then sauté for 4 minutes. Add uncooked rice and sauté for 2 minutes.

2. Add vegetable broth to the pot and bring to a boil. Cover and reduce heat. Cook for 20 minutes. Stir in black beans and spices. Serve.

Buttered Sirloin Steak

Serves 4

Calories: *453 calories per serving*

Ingredients:

- 2 lbs beef top sirloin steaks
- 1/4 cup butter
- 1 tsp. garlic powder
- 2 cloves garlic, minced
- salt and black pepper

Preparation:

1. Preheat grill to high heat. Meanwhile, generously season the steaks with salt and pepper.

2. Grill the steaks for 5 minutes on each side or until done to your liking.

3. While grilling steaks, combine butter, garlic powder and minced garlic in a saucepan over medium low heat.

4. Transfer steaks to serving plates and brush with garlic butter. Serve.

Baked Spinach and Pita

Serves 2

Calories: *350 calories per serving*

Ingredients:

- 2 6-in whole wheat pita breads
- 1/2 6-oz. tub sun-dried tomato pesto
- 1 Roma tomato, chopped
- 1/2 bunch spinach, chopped
- 1/4 cup fresh mushrooms, sliced
- 3 tbsp. feta cheese, crumbled
- 2 tbsp. Parmesan cheese, grated
- 1 tbsp. olive oil
- black pepper to taste

Preparation:

1. Preheat oven to 350 degrees F.

2. To assemble pita breads, spread tomato pesto on one side then top with tomatoes, mushrooms, spinach and cheeses. Drizzle with olive oil and add season with pepper.

3. Transfer to a baking sheet and bake for 12 minutes or until crisp. Cut and serve.

Baked & Buttered Haddock

Serves 4

Calories: *325 calories per serving*

Ingredients:

- 4 Haddock fillets
- 1/4 cup butter, melted
- 3/4 cup almond milk
- 3/4 cup bread crumbs
- 1/4 cup Parmesan cheese, grated
- 2 tsp. salt
- 1/4 tsp. ground dried thyme

Preparation:

1. Preheat oven to 500 degrees F.

2. In a bowl, whisk together salt and milk. In another bowl, combine bread crumbs, cheese and thyme.

3. Drip the fish fillets in the milk then coat with bread crumb mixture.

4. Transfer fish in a baking dish and drizzle with butter. Bake for about 15 minutes or until fish flakes.

Grilled Halibut Steaks

Serves 3

Calories: *275 calories per serving*

Ingredients:

- 1 lb halibut steak
- 2 tbsp. butter
- 2 tbsp. brown sugar

- 2 tsp. soy sauce
- 2 cloves garlic, minced
- 1 tbsp. lemon juice
- 1/2 tsp. ground black pepper

Preparation:

1. Preheat grill to medium high heat.

2. In a saucepan, combine butter, soy sauce, pepper, sugar, and garlic and lemon juice. Heat over medium heat while stirring occasionally until warm and sugar is dissolved.

3. Brush fish with sauce and place on oiled grill grates. Cook for 5 minutes for each side or until fish flakes easily.

Low Fat Pasta with Asparagus

Serves 2

Calories: *281 calories per serving*

Ingredients:

- 1/4 lb pasta
- 3/4 lb fresh asparagus, cut into 1-inch pieces
- 1/4 cup Parmesan cheese, grated
- 1/4 lb fresh mushrooms, sliced
- 2 tbsp. chicken broth
- 1 tsp. olive oil
- 1/4 tsp. red pepper, crushed

Preparation:

1. Cook pasta by following package instructions.

2. Heat the oil in a skillet and sauté asparagus for 3 minutes over medium heat. Add chicken broth and mushrooms. Continue cooking for another 3 minutes.

3. Drain pasta and transfer to a serving plate. Toss in asparagus and garnish with cheese and red pepper. Serve and enjoy!

Spicy Chicken with Mushrooms

Serves 4

Calories: *244 calories per serving*

Ingredients:

- 1 lb boneless chicken breast, cut in bite size pieces
- 1 cup chopped onions
- 1 cup fresh mushrooms
- 1 bunch fresh basil leaves
- 5 tbsp. oyster sauce
- 3 hot chili peppers
- 2 tbsp. chili oil
- 2 cloves garlic
- 1 tsp. black pepper
- 1 tsp. garlic powder
- 1 1/2 tsp. white sugar

Preparation:

1. In a skillet, heat oil and sauté garlic with chili peppers until brown. Add chicken, sugar, garlic powder and pepper. Cook until chicken is done.

2. Add oyster sauce then stir in mushrooms and onions. Continue cooking until onions are cooked. Remove from heat, add basil and let it sit for 2 minutes. Serve.

Trout Fillets in Foil

Serves 2

Calories: *213 calories per serving*

Ingredients:

- 2 trout fillets
- 2 tbsp. garlic salt
- 1 tbsp. olive oil
- 1 fresh jalapeno pepper, sliced
- 1 tsp. ground black pepper
- 1 lemon, sliced

Preparation:

1. Preheat oven to 400 degrees F.

2. Rinse and pat dry fish. Rub with olive oil then season with garlic salt and pepper.

3. Transfer fillet in a sheet of foil. Top with jalapeno pepper and squeeze with lemon juice.

4. Seal foil to enclose the fish and place in a baking dish. Bake for 15 to 20 minutes or until fish flakes.

Quick and Easy Garlic Pasta

Serves 4

Calories: *316 calories per serving*

Ingredients:

- 3/4 lb pasta
- 2 tbsp. Parmesan cheese, grated
- 2 tbsp. olive oil

- 1/2 clove garlic, crushed
- salt and black pepper to taste

Preparation:

5. Cook pasta according to package instructions.

6. Meanwhile, in a pan, heat oil and then add garlic. Sauté until browned.

7. Mix pasta and garlic then season with salt and pepper to taste. Finish off with Parmesan cheese and serve.

15-minute Tuna Melts

Serves 2

Calories: *236 calories per serving*

Ingredients:

- 1 whole wheat English muffin, split
- 1/2 6-oz can tuna, drained
- 6 slices picked jalapeno
- 2 slices Cheddar cheese
- 1/2 onion, minced
- pepper to taste

Preparation:

1. Preheat oven to 350 degrees F.

2. Combine tuna, pepper and onion in a bowl. Divide into 2 halves and top muffin slices. Add jalapeno slices on top then the cheddar cheese.

3. Place on a baking sheet and bake for 10 minutes.

Stir Fry Beef Asian-Style

Serves 4

Calories: *203 calories per serving*

Ingredients:

- 1 lb beef round steak, cut in strips
- 8 oz. snow peas
- 3 tbsp. soy sauce
- 2 tbsp. rice wine
- 1 tbsp. garlic, minced
- 1 tbsp. fresh ginger root, minced
- 1 tbsp. brown sugar
- 1 tbsp. olive oil
- 1/2 tsp. cornstarch

Preparation:

1. Combine sugar, wine, soy sauce and cornstarch in a bowl. Set aside.

2. In a skillet, heat oil over medium high heat. Add ginger and garlic and stir fry for 30 seconds. Stir in steak and cook for 2 minutes or until browned. Add snow peas and cook for another 3 minutes.

3. Stir in soy sauce mixture and bring to a boil. Reduce heat and simmer until sauce is thick. Serve with rice or mashed potatoes.

Broiled Herbed Chicken

Serves 2

Calories: *338 calories per serving*

Ingredients:

- 2 boneless chicken breasts, halves
- 1/4 cup butter, softened
- 1/2 tsp. dried parsley
- 1 clove garlic, minced
- 1/8 tsp. dried thyme
- 1/8 tsp. dried rosemary

Preparation:

1. Preheat oven to broil and prepare broiler pan by lining it with foil.

2. In a bowl, combine herbs, garlic and butter. Spread mixture on chicken breasts then transfer to pan.

3. Broil for about 15 minutes or until chicken juice is clear. Frequently turn and baste chicken with butter mix while broiling.

Steak and Spinach Salad with Walnuts

Serves 4

Calories: *310 calories per serving*

Ingredients:

- 1 lb top round steak, thinly sliced
- 6 cups fresh spinach, rinsed
- 1/2 cup walnut halves
- 1/2 cup dried cranberries
- 1 tomato, sliced
- salt and black pepper to taste

Preparation:

1. In a large plate, arrange dried spinach leaves. Spring with walnuts and cranberries then finish off with tomato slices. Set aside.

2. In a non-stick skillet, cook steak until no longer pink over medium heat.

3. Transfer steak on top of spinach salad. Season with salt and pepper to taste. Drizzle with salad dressing if desired.

Soups and Stews Recipes Ready Under 30 Minutes

Chicken Noodle Soup

Serves 4

Calories: *Under 200 calories per serving*

Ingredients:

- 1½ cup wide Egg noodles
- 1 tbsp. Butter
- ½ cup Onion, chopped
- ½ cup Celery, chopped
- ¾ cup Carrots, sliced
- 1½ cups Chicken meat
- 6 cups Chicken broth
- 1½ cups Vegetable broth
- ¼ cup Water
- ½ tsp. dried Basil
- ½ tsp. dried Oregano
- 1 tsp. Poultry seasoning
- 1 tsp. Salt
- Salt and pepper to taste

Preparation:

In a large pot, bring water to a boil. Add egg noodles and cook until tender. Drain and set aside. Melt butter in a large pot. Sauté onions and celery in butter until tender. Don't overcook. Add chicken, carrots, chicken broth, vegetable broth, water, basil, oregano, poultry seasoning, salt, and pepper. Bring to a boil then reduce heat and simmer for 15 minutes before serving.

Bean, Rice, and Chicken Stew

Serves 2

Calories: *Under 200-300 calories per serving*

Ingredients:

- 4 oz. Chicken breast, cooked skinless and boneless
- 2 cups Brown rice
- ½ cup Black or red beans, cooked
- ½ cup White onion, chopped
- 2 tsp. Ketchup
- 1 tsp. Dijon mustard
- 1 tsp. Worcestershire sauce
- ½ tsp. Brown sugar

Preparation:

Preheat oven to 350° F. Combine all ingredients in an oven-safe casserole dish and mix until everything is well combined. Bake in an uncovered dish for 25-30 minutes before serving.

Corn Chowder

Serves 4

Calories: *Under 250-300 calories per serving*

Ingredients:

- ½ cup Bacon
- 2 medium Potatoes, peeled and chopped
- ½ medium Onion, chopped
- 1½ cups Cream-style corn
- 1 cup Corn nibblets
- 1 cup Whole milk

- 1 cup Water
- 1 tsp. Salt
- Ground black pepper to taste

Preparation:

Cook bacon in a large pot until crisp then drain, but reserve 1 tbsp. bacon drippings in the pot. Crumble bacon in the pot then add the onions and potatoes. Stir well then cook for 5 minutes. Add water and season to taste with salt and pepper. Bring to a boil then reduce heat and simmer for 15 minutes. Cook until potatoes are tender. In a separate saucepan, warm the milk then add to the soup 5 minutes before serving.

Black Bean Soup

Serves 4

Calories: *Under 250-300 calories per serving*

Ingredients:

- 2 tbsp. Olive oil
- 1 medium size Onion, chopped
- 4 Garlic cloves, chopped
- 1 tbsp. Cumin
- 1 (15-oz.) can Black beans
- 3 Tomatoes, chopped
- 3½ cups Chicken broth
- 1 tbsp. Lime juice
- 1 tsp. Ground black pepper
- 1 tbsp. fresh Cilantro leaves

Preparation:

Heat olive oil in a large pan then add onions, garlic, and cumin. Sauté 3-5 minutes then add the rest of the ingredients except the cilantro. Bring to a boil then cover, reduce heat, and allow to simmer for 7 minutes. Add fresh cilantro and serve.

Sweet Potato Carrot Soup

Serves 4

Calories: *Under 200 calories per serving*

Ingredients:

- 1 tbsp. Olive oil or butter
- 1 medium Onion, chopped
- 1 Garlic clove, peeled and minced
- ½ tsp. Salt
- 1 Sweet potato, peeled and chopped
- 4 Carrots, peeled and chopped
- 1 tbsp. Ginger
- 1 cup low-sodium Chicken or vegetable stock,
- 2 cups Water
- ¼ cup Sour cream

Preparation:

Heat butter or oil in a pan then add onions, garlic, and salt. Sauté until onions are tender. Add sweet potato, carrots, ginger, water, and stock then bring to a boil. Reduce heat and simmer until vegetables are tender. Strain the vegetables then combine in a blender with the sour cream. Salt to taste before serving.

White Bean Soup

Serves 4

Calories: *Under 200 calories per serving*

Ingredients:

- 2 cups Cannellini beans
- 1 strip Bacon
- 4 tbsp. Olive oil
- 1 medium Onion, chopped
- 1½ stalks of Celery, finely chopped
- ½ Carrot, finely chopped
- 1 (15-oz.) can Plum or stewed tomatoes
- 1 (15-oz.) can Chicken or vegetable broth
- Salt and pepper to taste

Preparation:

1. Puree 1 cup of the beans in a food processor or blender and set aside., Cook bacon in a skillet until crispy and then crumble. In a separate pan, heat oil and sauté onions until tender. Add carrots, celery, tomatoes, and cook for 7 additional minutes.

2. Warm the broth then pour into the pan with the beans, bean puree, and bacon. Allow to simmer for 15 minutes then season with salt and pepper before serving.

Tomato Bisque Soup

Serves 4

Calories: *Under 200 calories per serving*

Ingredients:

- 2 Garlic cloves, peeled and minced
- 4 tbsp. Butter
- 3 tbsp. All-purpose flour
- 3 cups Chicken broth
- 9 oz. Tomato paste
- 1 tbsp. White sugar
- 1 tsp. Salt
- ¼ tsp. Ground pepper
- 1 Bay leaf
- ½ cup Half-and-half cream

Preparation:

Sauté garlic in a saucepan for 1-2 minutes. Add flour carefully while continuing to stir then slowly add the chicken broth. Add tomato paste and stir until well blended. Add sugar, salt, pepper, and bay leaf then bring mixture to a boil. Reduce heat and simmer. Slowly stir in the cream then remove bay leaf before serving.

Classic Lentil Soup

Serves 8

Calories: *300 calories per serving*

Ingredients:

- 1½ cups Red lentils, cooked
- 2 Celery stalks, chopped
- ½ cup Onion, chopped
- ½ medium Carrot, peeled and chopped
- 1 tsp. Dried oregano
- ½ cup Brown or white rice, cooked
- ½ cup fresh Parsley leaves, chopped
- 1 cup Tomatoes, chopped
- 10 cups Vegetable or chicken stock
- Salt and pepper to taste

Preparation:

Combine all ingredients in a large soup pot. Bring to a boil then reduce heat to low and cover. Simmer for 25 minutes until lentils are soft. Add salt and pepper to taste then serve.

Gazpacho Soup

Serves 4

Calories: *Under 200 calories per serving*

Ingredients:

- 3 Tomatoes, chopped
- 1 large Cucumber, chopped
- ½ Red onion, chopped
- 1 Yellow pepper, chopped
- 1 Garlic clove, minced
- 1 Celery stalk, chopped
- 1 tbsp. Extra-virgin olive oil
- 2 tbsp. Wine vinegar
- 2 tbsp. Lemon juice
- 3 cups Vegetable cocktail juice

Preparation:

Thoroughly combine all ingredients in a bowl and refrigerate for 3 hours until well chilled. Serve chilled.

Chickpea Soup

Serves 4

Calories: *Under 200 calories per serving*

Ingredients:

- 1 tbsp. Olive oil
- 1 Onion, chopped
- 1 Garlic clove, minced
- 2 Celery stalks, chopped
- 1 Green bell pepper, chopped
- 2 tsp. Rosemary leaves
- ½ tsp. dried Basil,
- 1 (15-oz.) can Tomato sauce
- 1 (15-oz.) can Chickpeas
- ½ tsp. dried Oregano
- ½ tsp. dried Parsley
- 4 cups Water
- Salt and pepper to taste

Preparation:

Heat olive oil over medium heat then sauté onion, garlic, celery, green pepper, rosemary, and basil for 5 minutes or until tender. Add tomato sauce, chickpeas, oregano, water, and parsley. Reduce heat to low and simmer for a few minutes then season with salt and pepper and serve.

Snacks

150-Calorie Snacks

- 15 Peanuts with 20 grapes
- ½ cup Dry cereal with 1 applesauce pouch
- 7 TLC Honey Sesame crackers with 1 mozzarella cheese stick
- 2 tbsp. Hummus with ½ large cucumber
- ½ cup Oat cereal with kiwi
- ¾ cup Edamame, steamed
- 3 Triscuits With sliced banana
- 1 cup Strawberries dipped in 1 tbsp. melted semisweet chocolate chips
- 6 Watermelon skewers each made with 1 slice cucumber, 1 cube watermelon, and 1 small cube feta cheese
- 45 or ½ cup Shelled pistachios
- 18 Rabbits bunny bar
- 1 tbsp. Peanut butter with 1 medium apple
- 3 tbsp. Hummus with 1 cup of snap peas
- 8 Kashi wheat thins with one light cheese wedge
- 3 Rye crackers with 1 tbsp. spreadable light cheese
- ¾ cup Strawberries with 1 oz. melted dark chocolate chips
- ½ cup Minestrone soup with 2 tsp. grated parmesan cheese
- Baby burrito made with 1 (6-inch) corn tortilla, 2 tbsp. bean dip, and 2 tbsp. salsa
- 1 packet Quaker's Instant Oatmeal
- ¼ cup Fresh pineapple with ¼ cup low-fat cottage cheese
- 7 Olives stuffed with 1 tbsp. blue cheese
- ½ cup Pumpkin seeds with or without shells
- 5 Brown rice vegetable sushi rolls
- 2 Graham cracker squares with 8 oz. skim milk
- 1 tsp. French's Honey Mustard and 1 oz. pretzels
- 1 medium apple, sliced with 4 turkey slices
- 1 small Baked potato topped with salsa
- ½ medium Avocado sprinkled with sea salt
- 15 salted Cashews
- 1 tbsp. Granola with 1 cup yogurt parfait
- 1 small container of Tapioca pudding

- 1 Skinny Cow Ice Cream Sandwich
- 15 Baked Tostitos Scoops with 2 tbsp. bean dip
- 1 medium Papaya with a squeeze of lime juice
- 10 Walnut halves and 1 kiwi, sliced
- ½ Whole-grain English muffin with 1 tbsp. peanut butter and sugar-free jelly
- 1 English muffin pizza made with 1 whole wheat English muffin with 1 tbsp. tomato sauce, 1 tbsp. parmesan cheese, and 1 tbsp. low-fat cheese
- ½ Bagel with Egg salad made with 1 whole egg, ½ tsp. low-fat mayo, and spices spread on half a toasted whole wheat bagel or ½ piece of whole wheat bread
- 5 Pitted dates stuffed with almonds
- ½ cup 1% Cottage cheese with 1 tbsp. almond butter
- 10 Baby carrots with 2 tbsp. light salad dressing
- ½ cup Fruit cup sorbet with ½ cup blueberries
- 1 Turkey wrap made with 2 pieces of deli turkey breast with 1 piece of whole grain flatbread, lettuce, tomatoes, and cucumbers
- 1 Quaker breakfast bar
- 1 Nabisco ginger snap cookie
- ½ Avocado
- ¾ cup Strawberries topped with 3 tbsp. Cool Whip
- 1 medium Mango
- 6 Dried figs
- Loaded pepper slices made with 1 cup of red bell pepper slices with ¼ cup warmed black beans and 1 tbsp. guacamole
- 1½ cup Watermelon, diced
- 1 small baked potato with salsa and 1 tbsp. low-fat cheese
- 2 frozen Fruit bars
- 1 can Tuna, drained
- ¾ cup Roasted cauliflower
- 4 Pot stickers with 2 tsp. reduced-sodium soy sauce
- ½ Peanut butter and jelly sandwich
- 1 Mother Earth crumble bar
- 25 frozen Red seedless grapes
- ½ cup Roasted chickpeas with 2 tbsp. olive oil
- 21 raw Almonds
- 12 Baked tortilla chips with ½ cup salsa
- Stuffed tomatoes made with 10 halved grape tomatoes with ¼ cup of ricotta cheese and 1 tbsp. diced black olives

- 2 tbsp. Hummus with 4 crackers
- ½ cup Applesauce with 10 pecan halves
- 1½ sticks Lowfat string cheese
- 2 oz. Turkey jerky
- ½ cup Instant oatmeal
- 2 scoops Sorbet
- ¼ cup Dried apricots
- Frozen banana slices
- 9 Chocolate-covered almonds
- 1 small cup Chocolate pudding
- 3 honey pretzels dipped in semisweet melted chocolate morsels
- 4 Chocolate chip cookies
- 50 Pepperidge Farm Crackers
- 9 Ritz crackers
- 12 Saltines
- 1 cup Grape tomatoes
- 5 Ritz crackers lightly smeared with peanut butter
- 4 Saltine jelly sandwiches
- ½ Blueberry muffin
- 1½ cups Frozen grapes
- 2 cups Air-popped popcorn with parmesan cheese
- 1 container of Jell-o Chocolate Fudge with 5 sliced strawberries
- Mediterranean salad made with 1 medium cucumber, 1 tomato, ½ red onion, and 2 tbsp. feta cheese
- 1 Large apple with cinnamon
- Watermelon treat made with 1 cup of diced watermelon with 2 tbsp. feta cheese
- Tasty pepper made with sliced bell pepper with salt and pepper marinated in 1 tbsp. balsamic vinegar
- 2 Vlasic Kosher Dill pickle spears
- 1 cup Cheerios
- Tuna salad made with 1 can of light tuna in water with 1 tbsp. low-fat mayo and 1 diced sweet pickle
- 1 Nestle Crunch reduced-fat ice-cream bar
- 2 Dole fruit juice bars
- ½ cup Breyers Light natural vanilla ice cream
- 2 popsicles
- 1 Quaker Chewy Peanut Butter and Chocolate Chunk granola bar
- 1/8 loaf Entenmann's Light Golden Loaf Cake
- 2 Fudgesicles

100-Calorie Snacks

- ½ frozen Banana dipped in melted dark chocolate
- Pineapple rounds, grilled or sautéed
- ½ cup Nonfat Greek yogurt with cinnamon and 1 tsp. honey
- 1 cup Blueberries with 2 tbsp. whipped topping
- 1 cup mixed Citrus-berry salad with 1 tbsp. fresh-squeezed orange juice
- 2 small dried Figs with 1 tbsp. low-fat ricotta cheese sprinkled with cinnamon
- 2 Graham cracker squares with 1 tsp. peanut butter sprinkled with cinnamon
- 10 Baby carrots with 2 tbsp. hummus
- 2 roasted Plum tomatoes topped with breadcrumbs and a sprinkle of parmesan cheese
- 1/3 cup Wasabi peas
- Cucumber sandwich made with ½ English muffin with 2 tbsp. cottage cheese and 3 slices of cucumber
- Kale chips made with ½ cup raw kale baked with 1 tsp. olive oil
- Cucumber salad made with 1 large Cucumber sliced with 2 tbsp. red onion and 2 tbsp. apple cider vinegar
- Chickpea salad made with ¼ cup of chickpeas, 1 tbsp. sliced scallions, a squeeze of lemon juice, and ¼ cup diced tomatoes
- 15 Mini pretzel sticks with 2 tbsp. fat-free cream cheese
- 40 Pepperidge Farm Goldfish
- ¼ cup Black beans with 1 tbsp. salsa and 1 tbsp. nonfat Greek yogurt
- 1 Nonfat mozzarella cheese stick with half of a baseball-sized apple
- ½ cup Nonfat cottage cheese with ½ cup fresh mango and pineapple
- 3 dried Apricots stuffed with 1 tbsp. crumbled blue cheese
- Strawberry salad made with 1 cup raw spinach, ½ cup diced strawberries, and 1 tsp. balsamic vinegar
- 1 cup Kale leaves with 1 tsp. honey and 1 tbsp. balsamic vinegar
- 4 slices Smoked turkey rolled up and dipped in 2 tbsp. honey mustard
- 1 Tomato, chopped and mixed with 1 tbsp. feta cheese and a squeeze of lemon juice
- ½ cup Raisin Bran
- 1½ cup Puffed rice
- ½ cup toasted Oat cereal
- 7 plain Animal crackers

- 1½ sheets of Graham crackers
- ½ sheet Matzo
- 25 Oyster crackers
- 7 Saltines
- 1 large raw Carrot
- ¾ cup cooked Carrot
- 2 stalks raw Celery
- 2 oz. Baked potato
- 1 raw Cucumber
- 1 cup Lettuce drizzled with 2 tbsp. fat-free dressing
- 6 Large clams
- ½ cup Potatoes mashed with milk and butter
- 2 oz. Baked potato
- ½ cup canned Crab
- 3 oz. fresh Crab, cooked
- 3 oz. Cod, cooked
- 1½ oz. Halibut, cooked
- 2 oz. Lobster, cooked
- 2 oz. Mussels, cooked
- 6 Oysters
- 2 oz. Salmon, cooked
- 2 oz. Salmon, smoked
- 2 oz. Scallops, cooked
- 4 large Scallops, cooked
- 2 oz. Yellowfin tuna, cooked
- 3 oz. Tuna, canned in water
- 14 Almonds
- 10 Cashews
- 2 tbsp. Flaxseeds
- 25 Dry-roasted peanuts
- 24 Oil-roasted peanuts
- 17 Pecans
- 2 tbsp. Poppy seeds
- 2 tbsp. Pumpkin seeds
- 2 tbsp. Sunflower seeds
- 6 Dried apricots
- 25 Cherries
- 1 cup Tomato bisque soup

- 3 Crackers lightly spread with butter
- 3 medium Breadsticks with hummus
- 1 Hard-boiled egg
- 2 small Peaches
- 1 cup Strawberries
- 1 small Baked potato
- 1 medium Corn on the cob with seasoning
- 30 Grapes
- ½ cup Unsweetened applesauce with 1 slice of whole-wheat toast
- 4-6 oz. Nonfat or low-fat yogurt
- 3 Pineapple rings in natural juices
- 3 Potato wedges, oven-baked
- 1 Rice cake with 1 tbsp. guacamole
- 1 cup Radishes
- 1 cup Fat-free and sugar-free yogurt
- 16 Artichokes
- 1 cup Zucchini, sliced
- 1 cup Chicken noodle soup
- ½ cup Clam chowder
- ¾ cup Minestrone soup
- 1 Nectarine
- ½ cup Sugar snap peas
- 2 slices Deli turkey breast
- 8 small Shrimp with 3 tbsp. cocktail sauce
- 1 tbsp. Peanuts with 2 tbsp. dried cranberries
- 1 cup Raspberries with 2 tbsp. plain yogurt
- 20 Olives
- 1 cup Miso soup
- 3 Celery sticks stuffed with carrots sticks
- Portabella mushrooms stuffed with 1 tsp. low-fat cheese and roasted veggies
- 1 medium Grapefruit with ½ tsp. sugar
- 6 Figs
- 20 Grapes with 15 peanuts
- ½ pound Fruit salad
- 4 Dates
- 1 small baked Sweet potato
- 1 fresh Pomegranate

- 2 cups Broccoli florets
- 1 stick Lowfat string cheese
- 3 Eggplant slices
- 3 oz. lean Roast beef,
- 1 Seven-grain Belgian waffle
- 4 Mini rice cakes with 2 tbsp. low-fat cottage cheese

Super SHRED Fruit Smoothies and Protein Shake Recipes Ready Under 30 Minutes

Blast of Super Protein Shake

Serves 2

Calories: *200-250 Calories per serving*

Ingredients:

- ¼ cup vanilla-flavored Whey protein powder
- 12 oz. Almond milk
- 4 Strawberries, fresh or frozen
- ¼ cup Blueberries, fresh or frozen
- 1 tsp. Honey
- 2 tbsp. Lowfat Vanilla yogurt
- 4 Ice cubes

Preparation:

Combine everything in a blender and mix on medium speed just long enough to incorporate the ingredients. Increase to high speed and blend until smooth and creamy.

Splash of the Tropics Protein Shake

Serves 2

Calories: *200 calories per serving*

Ingredients:

- ¼ cup vanilla-flavored Whey protein powder
- 1 cup Pineapple, frozen
- ¼ cup Blueberries, frozen
- ¾ cup unsweetened Almond vanilla milk
- 1 tbsp. unsweetened Coconut milk

Preparation:

Combine everything in a blender on medium speed to incorporate the ingredients then change to high speed until smooth and creamy.

Chocolate-y Protein Shake

Serves 1

Calories: *Under 200 Calories*

Ingredients:

- ¼ cup vanilla-flavored Whey protein powder
- 1 tsp. powdered Cocoa
- ½ Banana, sliced
- ¼ cup low-fat or skim Chocolate milk
- 4 Ice cubes

Preparation:

Combine everything in a blender on medium speed to incorporate the ingredients then increase to high until smooth and creamy.

Very Berry Protein Shake

Serves 2

Calories: *200-250 Calories per serving*

Ingredients:

- ¼ cup vanilla-flavored Whey protein powder
- 12 oz. Almond milk
- ¼ cup fresh or frozen Blackberries
- ¾ cup fresh or frozen Blueberries
- 2 tbsp. low-fat Vanilla yogurt
- ½ tbsp. Honey
- 4 Ice cubes

Preparation:

Combine everything in a blender on medium speed to incorporate the ingredients then increase to high until smooth and creamy.

Red Revolution Protein Shake

Serves 2

Calories: *200-250 calories per serving*

Ingredients:

- ¼ cup vanilla-flavored Whey protein powder
- 12 oz. Almond milk
- 4 fresh or frozen Strawberries
- ½ cup fresh or frozen Raspberries
- 2 tbsp. low-fat Vanilla yogurt
- 1 tsp. Sugar or ½ tsp. Agave nectar
- 4 Ice cubes

Preparation:

Combine everything in a blender on medium speed to incorporate the ingredients then increase to high until smooth and creamy.

Peach and Strawberry Smoothie

Serves 2

Calories: *Under 200 calories per serving*

Ingredients:

- ¼ cup vanilla-flavored Whey protein powder
- ½ cup (1 scoop) low-fat Vanilla ice cream,
- ½ cup fresh or frozen sliced strawberries with
- 1 small fresh peach, peeled and sliced
- 4 Ice cubes

Preparation:

Combine milk and ice cream in the blender then add fruit and ice and blend until smooth.

Creamy Delight Smoothie

Serves 1

Calories: *Under 200 calories*

Ingredients:

- ½ frozen Banana, peeled
- ½ cup frozen Strawberries
- 1½ tbsp. Flaxseed
- ½ cup fat-free plain Yogurt
- ½ cup Nonfat milk
- 1 tsp. Honey

Preparation:

Place all ingredients in a blender and mix until smooth and creamy.

Berry Lemon Smoothie

Serves 4

Calories: *Under 200 calories per serving*

Ingredients:

- 1 cup Blueberries
- 1 cup Strawberries
- 1 (8-oz.) container of nonfat Blueberry yogurt
- 1½ cups Skim milk
- 1 cup Ice cubes
- Juice from half a lemon

Preparation:

Place all ingredients in a blender and mix until smooth and creamy.

Easy-Peasy Mango Smoothie

Serves 1

Calories: *Under 200 calories*

Ingredients:

- ½ cup dried mangoes, diced and frozen
- 3 tbsp. low-fat plain Yogurt
- 2/3 cup Skim milk
- ½ tsp. Sugar or honey
- 4 Ice cubes

Preparation:

Place all ingredients in a blender and mix until smooth and creamy.

Berry-Orange Twist Smoothie

Serves 2

Calories: *Under 200 calories per serving*

Ingredients:

- 2 Navel oranges, peeled and cut into chunks
- 1 cup fresh or frozen Raspberries
- 1 cup fresh or frozen Blueberries
- ½ cup Plain yogurt
- ½ cup Ice

Preparation:

Place all ingredients in a blender and mix until smooth and creamy.

Sweet Detoxification Smoothie

Serves 2

Calories: *Under 200 calories per serving*

Ingredients:

- 2 cups Mixed frozen berries
- 1 Pear, peeled and sliced
- 1 cup unsweetened Pomegranate juice
- 1 cup Ice

Preparation:

Place all ingredients in a blender and mix until smooth and creamy.

Super Green Smoothie

Serves 2

Calories: *Under 200 calories per serving*

Ingredients:

- ½ cup Apple, peeled and chopped
- 4 Kale leaves
- ½ cup Mango, chopped
- 6 Romaine lettuce leaves
- ¼ cup fresh Parsley sprigs
- 1 inch fresh Ginger Root, peeled and chopped
- 1 cup Water

Preparation:

Place all ingredients in a blender and mix until smooth and creamy.

The Energizer Pear-Blueberry Smoothie

Serves 2

Calories: *Under 200 calories per serving*

Ingredients:

- 1½ whole Red pears
- 1 cup frozen Blueberries
- 1 cup plain low-fat Yogurt
- 1 tsp. Sugar
- 6 Ice cubes

Preparation:

Place all ingredients in a blender and mix until smooth and creamy.

Cucumber Delight Smoothie

Serves 2

Calories: *Under 200 calories per serving*

Ingredients:

- 1 large Garden cucumber
- ½ cup frozen Blueberries
- ½ cup plain or low-fat Yogurt
- ½ tbsp. Lemon juice
- ½ tbsp. Lime juice
- 1 tbsp. Honey

Preparation:

Place all ingredients in a blender and mix until smooth and creamy.

CHAPTER 2

The Super SHRED Diet Crash Course For Beginners

What Is The Super SHRED Diet?

The Super SHRED Diet is a revolutionary weight loss program that combines proper meal spacing, meal replacements, and exercise in order to improve health, reduce risk factors such as diabetes and heart problems, and of course, kick start weight loss. It combines a low GI diet that allows you to eat frequently over a period of four weeks.

Yes, you read that right – **It only takes four weeks for you to see significant results.** If you incorporate the program into your daily lifestyle, it can work for you like it did for thousands of people around the world.

But what's so special about the Super SHRED Diet anyway? And can it really deliver on its promise of giving you the best weight loss results possible? Read on to find out more, and you will soon be working your way towards a healthier, happier self!

How does the Super SHRED Diet Work?

The Super SHRED Diet was first conceptualized by Dr. Ian Smith who was the physician and fitness host who launched a national health initiative to help other people get fit. The idea of the Super SHRED diet is to work on a system that takes strategic dieting into account. This means that by sticking to a given, but not restrictive plan, you will be able to follow through and find success at the end of your journey.

In this diet regimen, you will be guided through four weeks with a different phase for each week in relation to your SHREDding goal. Note that adherence to the diet plan given to you is necessary for weight-loss success, and the menu can be customized based on your personal dietary restrictions or preferences. Substituting these recipes will not affect the results of the diet in any way.

The Super SHRED diet promises to be very easy to follow unlike most other diet plans that are so difficult to maintain long term. Because of its flexibility in recipes and menu planning combined with the exercise recommendations, you will be able to slip into the simple routine easily. Another great thing about the Super SHRED diet is that it creates a weekly goal for you to work on. By focusing on each goal, you direct all of your energy on a single mission until the next week comes to give you a new goal.

You may choose to stay on the program beyond four weeks, but every four weeks is considered a single cycle. The average weight loss for each cycle is estimated to be between 18-25 pounds although results may vary from person to person. For the first few weeks, the weight loss is rapid and builds up to a plateau mid-cycle. Then it begins slowing down as the cycle ends. This is expected to happen as your body grows accustomed to each new regimen. You can then choose to re-cycle if you find you haven't achieved your weight loss goal yet. You can re-cycle in a way that works best for you and your needs.

For every week of the Super SHRED diet, a specific goal is to be achieved. The goals in the proper order are Foundation, Accelerate, Shape, and Tenacious. Each cycle is designed as a pre-requisite to the following week, so skipping a week or two in order to jumpstart another goal is not recommended. The program includes a list of healthy and smart choices each week that are different from all other weeks. However, the end goal of all the weeks is to SHRED fat.

While adjusting to a new diet regimen is never easy, it is necessary to achieve the desired results. The secret to doing this successfully lies within you. It is important not to be too hard on yourself – especially if you find yourself stuck in a diet rut. No one is perfect, and bad days are inevitable. But you need to keep yourself focused on the end goal, so when the bad times come, remind yourself to hold on. It is best to find a diet partner to do this with so you can help each other out when it gets tough. Focus on what you want and what you need to achieve, and you will be able to carry through all the way to success.

This guide contains everything you need to know and what you need to do with that knowledge. You won't waste time over-thinking strategies on how to do it because this guide will guide you through each step of the way. As long as you follow the cycle in the step-by-step manner laid out, you'll be all set to reach your goal weight before you know it.

> "Sherri began the Super SHRED diet after she found herself always hungry and eating unhealthy things to satisfy that hunger. Once she started the program, she quickly discovered that making the right food choices made her healthier and happier with her physique as well. Now that she understands the essentials of meal spacing and substitutions that she learned with the SHRED diet, she doesn't feel that constant hunger that always demanded junk food."

Guidelines for a Successful SHRED Program

- Weigh yourself the morning you start the program, then don't weigh again until a week after you begin the diet.
- Small but frequent meals every 3-4 hours is crucial for this part. If you need to make substitutions, try to do so as little as possible. Looking at the week's menu ahead of time will help you make the proper substitutions while still keeping on track with the program.

- Do cardio exercises five times a week. You may choose to distribute the exercise sessions throughout the week, but make sure they add up to the total number of hours required for exercise that week.
- If you generally don't eat red or white meat, you can make appropriate substitutions using fish or vegetables.
- All shakes or smoothies must be less than 300 calories each with no added sugar.
- For soups, make sure each serving is less than 300 calories and low in sodium (less than 480 mg). Using sea salt to personal taste is best. You can also eat soups with saltine crackers.
- Liquid meals must be eaten with one serving of vegetables or one piece of fruit.
- You need to drink one cup of water before each meal, and one cup of water during each meal. Try adding a lemon or lime for flavor or substitute fizzy water instead.
- You are allowed one cup of coffee per day, but make sure it only has 50 calories. You also should avoid fancy coffee preparations as those are usually much higher in calories.
- Make sure you eat your last meal at least 90 minutes before bedtime.
- Before going to bed, you can eat a 100-calorie snack if desired.
- Use healthy snack options and refrain from eating doughnuts, candies, and any other preserved or artificial sweets.
- You don't have to eat everything on the day's menu, but make sure you don't skip or double up meals, or exceed their measured guidelines in size and volume.
- Condiments such as soy sauce, mustard, ketchup, etc. are limited to no more than one teaspoon with each meal.
- Spices, on the other hand, are unlimited.
- You may choose to eat canned fruit, but remember that fresh fruit is better. Canned vegetables may also be eaten, but make sure to choose those that are low in sodium.
- You are allowed to drink an unlimited amount of water every day. Make sure you don't drink soda although one can of diet soda a day is allowed.
- Flavored waters and sports drinks must be less than 60 calories.
- When it comes to drinking alcohol, you are allowed three light beers, one mixed drink, or three regular glasses of red or white wine per week.

4 Phases of the SUPER SHRED Diet

Week 1: Foundation

This is the week you begin your induction into the Super SHRED diet program. During this week you will be oriented to meal spacing, snacking, and learning how to consume the right snacks to suppress hunger without consuming too many calories. You can expect to lose around 3.5 pounds in this phase and even more if you are 20 pounds or more over your ideal weight. The farther away from your target weight you are, the more weight you will lose in week one.

Meal spacing is a crucial part of the Super SHRED diet. Always remember that what you eat, how much you consume, and the calories in your food are all things that need to be considered in depth for successful meal planning. These factors will have an impact on how much weight you lose depending on how much you consume and when. In order to get the most out of a weight loss regimen, proper meal spacing is needed. A regular meal consumed in small increments can help control hormone levels and keep blood sugar levels balanced so spikes in hunger leading to overconsumption can be avoided.

Another important principle addressed in the Super SHRED diet is what we call "diet confusion". This is very similar to the concept of muscle confusion in the sense that its goal is to keep the body guessing in hopes of making it more efficient. To provide a clearer picture, consider the basis of a daily workout. For example, when you do repetitive exercises such as weight lifting, your body will eventually get used to it. As your body becomes familiar with the exercises in the long run, it will stop responding properly to familiar exercise routines and intensity levels. Your muscles which have changed due to your hard exercise will cease to be "impressed" enough to continue to change by the same workout routines. This means you need to perform a variety of exercises throughout the week in order to keep your body surprised and responding the way you want it to in order to lose weight.

This same concept can be applied to dieting. If you stick to a particular set of ingredients or a specific menu for a long period of time, your digestive track will become very familiar with digesting them. This is a good thing in general, but not when it comes to weight loss because that increase in efficient familiarity leads to less energy spent on digestion which ultimately results in fewer calories burned. By varying your food choices, you keep your body guessing which increases your metabolism and burns more fat for each new set of food. The main purpose is really to rescue you from food boredom while increasing your metabolism at the same time.

Super SHRED is more than just a diet program – it is a lifestyle program. This is best illustrated by its emphasis on exercise. Dieting is just one part of the equation. In order for any diet to be successful, you must do your part to get rid of the unwanted weight. The goal is to develop lean muscle mass in order to increase metabolism. This can be achieved through resistance training. Why is an increase in metabolism so important anyway? Well, once your metabolism rate increases, you will be able to burn more calories, reduce risks for heart disease and diabetes, improve flexibility, and increase blood flow.

The plan is designed to give you flexibility for doing the exercises you need in particular. Once you get used to a certain exercise, you have the freedom to break it up into smaller sessions. As long as you are able to add up the time required for each exercise, it doesn't matter if you do it short increments. The important thing is to focus on the intensity. The more intensely you exercise, the faster you will achieve your weight loss goals. In the first cycle of the Super SHRED diet, you are asked to do almost all cardio workouts.

Here are some exercise guidelines for the week:

- Cardio exercise in 15-minute intervals for a total of 45 minutes minimum. If you want to do more, it's completely up to you!
- Jogging outside, walking/running on a treadmill, elliptical machine, stationary or mobile bicycle, swimming laps, rowing machine, stair climbing, 225 jump rope revolutions, treadmill walk/run intervals, Zumba, or other type of aerobics, spinning classes, or high-intensity cardio programs.

A significant part of any diet is food. But what's unique to the Super SHRED diet is that it allows flexibility in your food choices. The Super SHRED diet considers your preferences, medical conditions, allergies, and any other factors that prevent you from eating or drinking a particular type of food or beverage.

Week 2: Accelerate

The focus of Week 2 is Accelerate which means you need to kick it up and speed up the weight loss. During this week, you not only address the physical demands of the regimen, but more importantly, you also address your mental and emotional struggles. This phase is just an accelerated version of your first week. It takes a lot of confidence to rise to the challenge of sticking with a new diet program, and this week is dedicated to helping you boost your own much-needed self-esteem. By this time you will have developed self-awareness and a strong sense of purpose, and you will find yourself slowly easing into the program which helps you prepare for the weeks ahead. Your exercise recommendation for this cycle involves weight lifting or any other type of resistance training. Resistance training helps you build lean muscle mass in order to increase metabolism, build bone density and strength, and prevent various diseases or medical conditions. In addition to your 20 minutes of resistance work, you should also do cardio training 2-3 times per week. This week, your shakes, soups, and smoothies must be less than 250 calories each.

Week 2 teaches that despite the failures you may have encountered in the past, you now have the right tools to be successful.

Each day's exercise is expected to be for at least 45 minutes minimum, but you can choose to continue your workout after that if you wish to do so.

Week 3: Shape

The third week is all about Shape, and this is when you will begin to notice positive changes. This is also notably the toughest week you will ever encounter, because it will help get your body back by keeping it guessing. By the end of the week, you should start seeing increased energy levels and decreased clothing sizes. This is also the crucial time when you will have the most positive mindset and the best overall outlook about the rest of the program. Although it is designed to be the toughest week, you will feel like there is nothing too tough to handle. However, knowing this fact is only part of the process. The other part is to keep working and get through the entirety of the SHRED regimen. You also need to visualize your body continually SHREDding off fat which will help you stay on course.

Each day's exercise is for a minimum of 40 minutes, but you can choose to keep exercising as tolerated. The first session should be done before 12 pm and the second one after 2 pm.

Week 4: Tenacious

After the darkest week has passed, you are now on your fourth week. As you begin your ascent out of the toughest week, you are ready to emerge with a renewed sense of confidence for the fourth week of the diet. You should expect to keep working hard, but since you've tackled and survived the worst part, it won't be as hard for you anymore. At this time you will feel re-energized to get on with this last phase of the Super SHRED program. According to the proponent of the Super SHRED diet, this is the merging of week 4 and week 6 from the regular SHRED diet. The only thing that's been left out in this fast-track way to SHREDding is the former Week 5, which focuses on detoxification. You are now on your last week of a very productive weight loss program, and your improved eating habits as well as your final sprint at this helps melt off those stubborn last pounds.

Each day's exercise should be for a minimum of 30 minutes, but again, you can choose to continue your workout as tolerated.

You may opt to do a combination of the following exercises:

- 15 minutes jogging
- 15 minutes walking/treadmill
- 15 minutes on elliptical machine
- 15 minutes on stationary or mobile bike
- 15 minutes swimming laps
- 15 minutes on stair climber
- 225 jump rope revolutions
- 20 minutes treadmill intervals
- 15 minutes Zumba
- 15 minutes spinning
- 15 minutes any other high-intensity cardio
- 15 minutes rowing machine

Additional guidelines for this week include:

- Alcohol allowed in moderation.
- You may also consume two slices of whole wheat or whole grain bread throughout the day.

How does ending the cycle with a bang sound? Well, that's exactly what should happen this final week of the program. For some people this week signifies the final success of reaching their ideal weight, but that may not be the case for other people. But remember – the SHRED cycle is meant to be repeated until you're satisfied with your weight loss. By now the newly formed habits from the previous weeks will easily incorporate into your lifestyle without a whole lot of extra thought or effort necessary. You will have learned the purpose of the SHRED diet and how it isn't just used to get rid of excess weight. It is also to get you to a place where it's no longer just a diet, but a lifestyle to follow in order to stay healthy. You can stop looking at your notes and taking advice from the program at this point because the meal spacing and exercise regimens will have become second nature to you. Now you have developed a new way of living that is naturally healthy and guilt-free.

"Pete has been on the Super SHRED diet for a while, and he states that the diet works for him because it speeds up his metabolism by not "boring" his stomach by eating the same foods every day. With the wide variety of good food options, his body entered what is called "diet confusion" where the stomach more effectively metabolizes food by virtue of unfamiliarity. The effects are not limited to his figure, but they also contributed to a healthier immune system along with a significant improvement with his previous blood sugar problems."

CHAPTER 3

Jumpstart Your Super SHRED Diet!

7-Day Sample Meal Template

Now that you've gained the basic knowledge of how to follow the Super SHRED diet and have the recipes that you need to do so, it is time to make a comprehensive plan in order to rotate your meals properly.

This is how you are expected to space your meals throughout the day:

8:30 AM	Meal 1
10:00 AM	Snack 1
11:30 AM	Meal 2
1:00 PM	Snack 2
3:30 PM	Meal 3
7:00 PM	Meal 4
8:30 PM	Snack 3

Sample Weekly Menu:

Week 1, Day 1

Meal 1:

- 1 piece of Fruit
- Choose one of the following: 1½ cups cooked oatmeal, 2 eggs or 1 egg-white omelet with diced vegetables, 1 small bowl sugar-free cereal, or 1 container of low-fat yogurt.
- 1 cup fresh Juice

Snack 1:

- Less than 100 calories

Meal 2:

- Choose one of the following (not to exceed 300 calories): 1 fruit smoothie, 1 protein shake, or 1 bowl of soup without meat, cream, or potatoes.
- 1 serving of vegetables or 1 piece of fruit
- Choose one of the following beverages: 1 (12-oz.) can of diet soda, 1 cup fresh lemonade, 1 cup flavored water, 1 cup fresh juice, 1 cup unsweetened tea, or 1 cup low-fat, unsweetened soy or almond milk, and unlimited plain water.

Snack 2:

- Less than 150 calories

Meal 3:

- 1 small salad without bacon bits, croutons, and a maximum of 3 tbsp. fat-free dressing
- Choose one of the following: 1 piece of chicken (4-6 oz., no skin & not fried), 1 piece turkey (4-6 oz., no skin & not fried), or 1 piece of fish (4-6 oz., not fried)
- 1 slice of cheese
- 1 serving of vegetables
- Choose one from any of the following beverages: 1 (12 oz.) can of diet soda, 1 cup fresh lemonade, 1 cup flavored water, 1 cup fresh juice, 1 cup unsweetened tea, or 1 cup low-fat, unsweetened soy or almond milk, and unlimited plain water.

Meal 4:

- 3 servings of vegetables
- 1 cup Beans, not baked
- Choose one from any of the following beverages: 1 (12 oz.) can of diet soda, 1 cup fresh lemonade, 1 cup flavored water, 1 cup fresh juice, 1 cup unsweetened tea, or 1 cup low-fat, unsweetened soy or almond milk, and unlimited plain water.

Snack 3:

- Less than 100 calories

Exercise:

- Cardio exercises in 15-minute intervals for a total of 30 minutes a day minimum. If you want to do more, it's up to you!

Week 1, Day 2

Meal 1:

- 1 piece of Fruit (pear, grapefruit, or apple)
- Choose one of the following: 1½ cups cooked oatmeal, 2 egg whites or 1 egg-white omelet with diced vegetables, 1 small bowl sugar-free cereal, or 1 container of low-fat yogurt.
- 1 piece whole grain bread or whole wheat toast
- 1 cup fresh grapefruit, apple, orange, carrot, pear, or tomato juice

Snack 1:

- Less than 100 calories

Meal 2:

- 1 chicken or turkey sandwich on whole wheat or whole grain bread with tomato, lettuce, 1 slice of cheese, and 1 tsp. of mustard or mayo. You can also substitute the meal with a medium salad.
- Choose one of the following beverages: 1 (12 oz.) can of diet soda, 1 cup fresh lemonade, 1 cup flavored water, 1 cup fresh juice, 1 cup unsweetened tea, or 1 cup low-fat, unsweetened soy or almond milk, and unlimited plain water.

Snack 2:

- Less than 150 calories

Meal 3:

- Choose one from any of the following and make sure each serving is less than 300 Calories: 1 fruit smoothie, 1 protein shake, or 1 bowl of soup without potatoes or cream such as chicken noodle, lentil, vegetable, split pea, chickpea, tomato bisque, or black bean.
- 1 serving of vegetables or 1 piece of fruit

- Choose one from any of the following beverages: 1 (12 oz.) can of diet soda, 1 cup fresh lemonade, 1 cup flavored water, 1 cup fresh juice, 1 cup unsweetened tea, or 1 cup low-fat, unsweetened soy or almond milk, and unlimited plain water.

Snack 3:
- Less than 100 calories

Meal 4:
- 2 servings of vegetables
- 1 cup Beans, not baked
- Choose one of the following: 1 piece of chicken (4-6 oz., no skin & not fried), 1 piece turkey (4-6 oz., no skin & not fried), or 1 piece of fish (4-6 oz., not fried)
- Choose one from any of the following beverages: 1 (12 oz.) can of diet soda, 1 cup fresh lemonade, 1 cup flavored water, 1 cup fresh juice, 1 cup unsweetened tea, or 1 cup low-fat, unsweetened soy or almond milk, and unlimited plain water.

Exercise:
- Cardio exercises in 15-minute intervals for a total of 45 minutes a day minimum. If you want to do more, it's up to you!

Week 1, Day 3

Meal 1:
- 1 piece of Fruit (pear or grapefruit)
- Choose one of the following: 1½ cups cooked oatmeal, 2 egg whites or 1 egg-white omelets with diced vegetables, 1 small bowl sugar-free cereal, 1 container of low-fat yogurt, 2 pancakes plus 2 strips of turkey bacon with 1 pat of butter and no more than 1½ tsp. of syrup, or 1 small bowl of Cream of Wheat cereal.
- 1 cup fresh grapefruit, apple, orange, carrot, pear, or tomato juice

Snack 1:
- Less than 100 calories

Meal 2:

- Choose one from any one of the following but make sure each serving is less than 300 Calories: 1 fruit smoothie, 1 protein shake, or 1 bowl of soup without potatoes or cream such as chicken noodle, lentil, vegetable, split pea, chickpea, tomato bisque, or black bean.
- Choose one of the following beverages: 1 (12 oz.) can of diet soda, 1 cup fresh lemonade, 1 cup flavored water, 1 cup fresh juice, 1 cup unsweetened tea, or 1 cup low-fat, unsweetened soy or almond milk, and unlimited plain water.

Snack 2:

- Less than 150 calories

Meal 3:

- 1 chicken or turkey sandwich on whole wheat or whole grain bread with tomato, lettuce, 1 slice of cheese, and 1 tsp. of mustard or mayo. You can also substitute the meal with a medium salad.
- 1 serving of vegetables or 1 piece of fruit
- Choose one from any of the following beverages: 1 (12 oz.) can of diet soda, 1 cup fresh lemonade, 1 cup flavored water, 1 cup fresh juice, 1 cup unsweetened tea, or 1 cup low-fat, unsweetened soy or almond milk, and unlimited plain water.

Snack 3:

- Less than 100 calories

Meal 4:

- 1 serving of vegetables
- ½ cup brown rice
- Choose one of the following: 1 piece of chicken (4-6 oz., no skin &, not fried), 1 piece turkey (4-6 oz., no skin & not fried), or 1 piece of fish (4-6 oz., not fried)
- Choose one from any of the following beverages: 1 (12 oz.) can of diet soda, 1 cup fresh lemonade, 1 cup flavored water, 1 cup fresh juice, 1 cup unsweetened tea, or 1 cup low-fat, unsweetened soy or almond milk, and unlimited plain water.

Exercise:

■ Today is your rest day so take a break! However, you are allowed to exercise if you want to, but make sure to stay within the recommended guidelines. You may find it helpful to take up a sport in order to keep burning calories without it feeling like a work out.

Week 1, Day 4

Meal 1:

■ 1 piece of Fruit (pear or grapefruit)
■ Choose one of the following: 1½ cups cooked oatmeal, 2 egg whites or 1 egg-white omelet with diced vegetables, 1 small bowl sugar-free , 1 container of low-fat yogurt, or 1 grilled cheese sandwich on a whole wheat bread.
■ 1 cup fresh grapefruit, apple, orange, carrot, pear, or tomato juice

Snack 1:

■ Less than 100 calories

Meal 2:

■ 1 bowl of soup without potatoes or cream such as chicken noodle, lentil, vegetable, split pea, chickpea, tomato bisque, or black bean.
■ 1 small green salad
■ Choose one of the following beverages: 1 (12 oz.) can of diet soda, 1 cup fresh lemonade, 1 cup flavored water, 1 cup fresh juice, 1 cup unsweetened tea, or 1 cup low-fat, unsweetened soy or almond milk, and unlimited plain water.

Snack 2:

■ Less than 150 calories

Meal 3:

■ 1 protein shake or fruit smoothie
■ 1 serving of vegetables or 1 piece of fruit
■ Choose one from any of the following beverages: 1 (12 oz.) can of diet soda, 1 cup fresh lemonade, 1 cup flavored water, 1 cup fresh juice, 1 cup unsweetened tea, or 1 cup low-fat, unsweetened soy or almond milk, and unlimited plain water.

Snack 3:

- Less than 100 calories

Meal 4:

- 1 servings of vegetables
- Choose one of the following: 5 oz. of lean beef, 5 oz. of chicken, 5 oz. of fish, or 5 oz. of turkey (no skin and not fried)
- ½ Sweet potato
- Choose one from any of the following beverages: 1 (12 oz.) can of diet soda, 1 cup fresh lemonade, 1 cup flavored water, 1 cup fresh juice, 1 cup unsweetened tea, or 1 cup low-fat, unsweetened soy or almond milk, and unlimited plain water.

Exercise:

- Today's exercise is for a minimum of 40 minutes, but you can choose to continue your workout as long as tolerated.

Week 1, Day 5

Meal 1:

- 1 piece of Fruit (choose a different fruit from yesterday)
- Choose one of the following: 1½ cups cooked oatmeal, 2 egg whites or 1 egg-white omelets with diced vegetables, 1 small bowl sugar-free cereal, or 1 container of low-fat yogurt
- 1 cup fresh grapefruit, apple, orange, carrot, pear, or tomato juice

Snack 1:

- Less than 100 calories

Meal 2:

- 1 protein shake or fruit smoothie
- 1 serving of vegetables or fruit
- Choose one of the following beverages: 1 (12 oz.) can of diet soda, 1 cup fresh lemonade, 1 cup flavored water, 1 cup fresh juice, 1 cup unsweetened tea, 1 cup low-fat, unsweetened soy or almond milk, and unlimited plain water.

Snack 2:

- Less than 150 calories

Meal 3:

- 1 small garden salad
- 1 serving of vegetables or 1 piece of fruit
- 1 bowl of soup without potatoes or cream such as chicken noodle, lentil, vegetable, split pea, chickpea, tomato bisque, or black bean.
- Choose one from any of the following beverages: 1 (12 oz.) can of diet soda, 1 cup fresh lemonade, 1 cup flavored water, 1 cup fresh juice, 1 cup unsweetened tea, or 1 cup low-fat, unsweetened soy or almond milk, and unlimited plain water.

Snack 3:

- Less than 100 calories

Meal 4:

- 2 servings of vegetables
- Choose one of the following: 5 oz. of lean beef, 5 oz. of chicken, 5 oz. of fish, or 5 oz. of turkey (no skin and not fried)
- Choose one from any of the following beverages: 1 (12 oz.) can of diet soda, 1 cup fresh lemonade, 1 cup flavored water, 1 cup fresh juice, 1 cup unsweetened tea, or 1 cup low-fat, unsweetened soy or almond milk, and unlimited plain water.

Exercise:

- Today's exercise is for a minimum of 40 minutes, but you can choose to continue your workout as tolerated.

Week 1, Day 6

Meal 1:

- 1 piece of Fruit (choose a different fruit from yesterday)
- Choose one of the following: 1½ cups cooked oatmeal, 2 egg whites or 1 egg-white omelet with diced vegetables, 1 small bowl sugar-free cereal, 1 container of low-fat yogurt, or 1 piece grilled cheese sandwich on whole wheat bread.
- 1 cup fresh grapefruit, apple, orange, carrot, pear, or tomato juice

Snack 1:
- Less than 150 calories

Meal 2:
- 1 protein shake or fruit smoothie, or 1 bowl of soup without potatoes or cream such as chicken noodle, lentil, vegetable, split pea, chickpea, tomato bisque, or black bean.
- 1 serving of vegetables or fruit
- Choose one of the following beverages: 1 (12 oz.) can of diet soda, 1 cup fresh lemonade, 1 cup flavored water, 1 cup fresh juice, 1 cup unsweetened tea, or 1 cup low-fat, unsweetened soy or almond milk, and unlimited plain water.

Snack 2:
- Less than 100 calories

Meal 3:
- 1 small garden salad
- ½ cup brown or white rice
- Choose one of the following: 1 piece of chicken (4-6 oz., no skin & not fried), 1 piece turkey (4-6 oz., no skin & not fried), or 1 piece of fish (4-6 oz., not fried)
- Choose one from any of the following beverages: 1 (12 oz.) can of diet soda, 1 cup fresh lemonade, 1 cup flavored water, 1 cup fresh juice, 1 cup unsweetened tea, or 1 cup low-fat, unsweetened soy or almond milk, and unlimited plain water.

Snack 3:
- Less than 100 calories

Meal 4:
- 1 large green salad
- 1 cup of lentils, beans, chickpeas, or any other legumes
- Choose one from any of the following beverages: 1 (12 oz.) can of diet soda, 1 cup fresh lemonade, 1 cup flavored water, 1 cup fresh juice, 1 cup unsweetened tea, or 1 cup low-fat, unsweetened soy or almond milk, and unlimited plain water.

Snack 4:

Choose one of the following:
- ½ cup raw trail mix
- 2 Dates stuffed with almonds
- ½ cup walnuts, raisins, and a pinch of sea salt
- 3 slices of tomato with fresh basil drizzled with olive oil
- ½ sliced cucumber sprinkled with sea salt and drizzled with vinaigrette dressing
- 1 cup unsweetened apple sauce
- Assortment of nuts and 10 cherries
- 2 tbsp. hummus with 8 baby carrots
- 2 celery sticks with 1 tbsp. raw nut butter and 1 tbsp. organic raisins
- 1 medium sized piece fruit
- Small beet salad
- 1 cup Beet juice
- 20 Almonds
- small Fruit cup
- 8 dried Apricots halves
- 2 tbsp. Sunflower seeds,
- 4 slices of whole grain or Melba whole wheat toast

Exercise:

- Today is your rest day so take a break! However, if you want to exercise, it's allowed, but make sure you follow the recommended guidelines. You may find it helpful to take up a sport in order to keep burning calories without it feeling like a work out.

Week 1, Day 7

Meal 1:

- 1 piece of Fruit (choose a different fruit from yesterday)
- Choose one of the following: 1½ cups cooked oatmeal, 2 egg whites or 1 egg-white omelets with diced vegetables, 1 small bowl sugar-free cereal, or 1 container of low-fat yogurt
- 1 cup fresh grapefruit, apple, orange, carrot, pear, or tomato juice

Snack 1:

- Less than 100 calories

Meal 2:

- 1 protein shake or fruit smoothie, or 1 bowl of soup without potatoes or cream such as chicken noodle, lentil, vegetable, split pea, chickpea, tomato bisque, or black bean.
- 1 serving of vegetables or fruit
- Choose one of the following beverages: 1 (12 oz.) can of diet soda, 1 cup fresh lemonade, 1 cup flavored water, 1 cup fresh juice, 1 cup unsweetened tea, or 1 cup low-fat, unsweetened soy or almond milk, and unlimited plain water

Snack 2:

- Less than 150 calories

Meal 3:

- 1 small garden salad
- 1 piece of fruit
- Choose one from any of the following beverages: 1 (12 oz.) can of diet soda, 1 cup fresh lemonade, 1 cup flavored water, 1 cup fresh juice, 1 cup unsweetened tea, or 1 cup low-fat, unsweetened soy or almond milk, and unlimited plain water.

Snack 3:

- Less than 100 calories

Meal 4:

- 1 large green salad
- Choose one of the following: 5 oz. of lean beef, 5 oz. of chicken, 5 oz. of fish, or 5 oz. of turkey (no skin and no frying for any meat)
- Choose one from any of the following beverages: 1 (12 oz.) can of diet soda, 1 cup fresh lemonade, 1 cup flavored water, 1 cup fresh juice, 1 cup unsweetened tea, or 1 cup low-fat, unsweetened soy or almond milk, and unlimited plain water.

Exercise:

- Today's exercise is for a minimum of 40 minutes, but you can choose to continue your workout as tolerated. Ideally, you should complete today's workout in two sessions – one before 12 pm and the other after 2 pm.

Preparing Yourself

The first step is to have the right mindset. Answer the following questions and take your own self-awareness quiz to help guide you in setting the right goals that will allow you to lose the desire amount of weight.

Answer these questions on a blank piece of paper:

1. What is your current diet composed of?

2. What are your ideal outcomes for following the Super SHRED Diet?

3. What are the health concerns that you want to address in following this program?

4. How will this program benefit you?

5. What are the things you can do to help yourself keep the commitments involved when following this diet plan?

Your Daily Motivation Guide

Answer these questions on a blank piece of paper:

1. Today I will keep myself healthy by sticking to the Super SHRED diet. In order to do this, I will…

2. I am doing this for my health because I want to…

Conclusion

Congratulations to the successful Super SHREDder! You are now to the point where after completing a six-week cycle, you will have developed new eating and exercise habits.

The goal of the Super SHRED diet is to push you to incorporate these helpful habits for the long term. Each week of the cycle is an important leg of preparation for the next stage.

As a Super SHREDder, you can now fully engage in a healthier lifestyle, and because the Super SHRED diet slowly eases you into it instead of forcing it with strict and drastic regulations, you will stop feeling like you're on a diet!

Bear in mind that you can always fall back on this flexible program for maintenance as needed. Be positive – a greater life and increased vitality is now within reach!

Finally, if you enjoyed this guide, please take the time to share what you like about this guide and post a review on Amazon. It'd be greatly appreciated!

Thank you and good luck!

— Sharon Stewart

Check Out Other Books

Below you'll find some of the other popular books that are popular on Amazon and Kindle as well. Simply click on the links below to check them out.

Slow Cooker Recipes Quick & Easy Cookbook - Mouthwatering Recipes Prepared in 30 Minutes or Less!

http://amzn.to/1kaxG9W

High Protein Low Carb Diet - Lose Weight Effortlessly & Permanently

http://amzn.to/1dBDxxu

Atkins Diet Recipes Under 30 Minutes - Over 30 Atkins Recipes For All Phases (Includes Atkins Induction Recipes)

http://amzn.to/NyfMA5

Made in the USA
Lexington, KY
12 March 2015